THIS LAND CALLED AMERICA: **SOUTH CAROLINA**

CREATIVE EDUCATION

Published by Creative Education
P.O. Box 227, Mankato, Minnesota 56002
Creative Education is an imprint of The Creative Company
www.thecreativecompany.us

Design by Blue Design (www.bluedes.com)
Art direction by Rita Marshall
Book production by The Design Lab
Printed in the United States of America

Photographs by Alamy (Pat & Chuck Blackley, Danita Delimont, Buddy Mays,
North Wind Picture Archives), Corbis (Bettmann, Terry Cryer, Kim Hart/
Robert Harding World Imagery, Historical Picture Archive, Chris Keane/
Reuters, Bob Krist, Reuters, Michael T. Sedam, Stapleton Collection), Getty
Images (Altrendo Nature, Terry Ashe//Time & Life Pictures, Todd Bennett,
Albert Chau/FilmMagic, Ed Clark//Time & Life Pictures, Jon Ferrey/Allsport,
FPG/Hulton Archive, Eric Horan, Will McIntyre//Time & Life Pictures),
iStockphoto (Sondra Paulson)

Library of Congress Cataloging-in-Publication Data
Gilbert, Sara:
South Carolina / by Sara Gilbert.
p. cm. — (This land called America)
Includes bibliographical references and index.
ISBN 978-1-58341-793-5
1. South Carolina—Juvenile literature. I. Title. II. Series.
F269.3.G55 2009
975.7—dc22   2008009520

First Edition
9 8 7 6 5 4 3 2 1

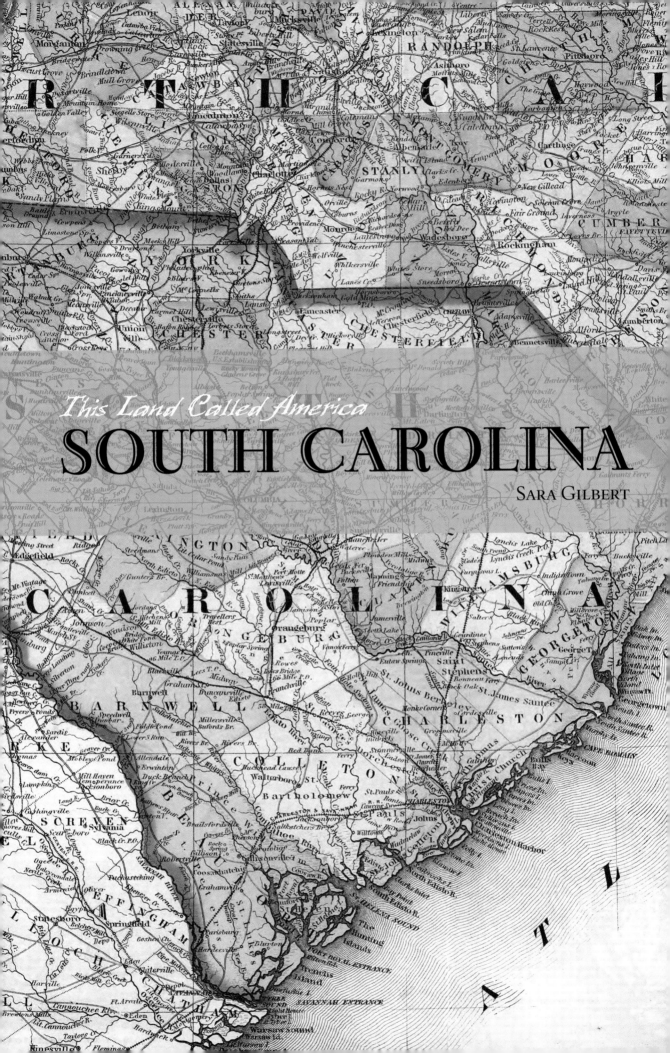

This Land Called America

SOUTH CAROLINA

Sara Gilbert

South Carolina

SARA GILBERT

Sparkling blue waves splash onto the soft white sand. Each wave mixes with the laughter of families playing in the Atlantic Ocean. From early spring until late fall, South Carolina's beaches are the perfect playground for kids of all ages. While children collect shells, parents sit in the shade of colorful umbrellas. Joggers run along the shore. Swimmers bob up and down in the water. Lush green golf courses are nearby. Fresh shrimp, oysters, and crabs are available at restaurants all along the shore. But for many in South Carolina, it's almost impossible to resist the pull of the beach.

Spanish explorers establish the first European settlement in the U.S. at San Miguel de Guadalupe.

War and Peace

SPANISH EXPLORERS FIRST VISITED SOUTH CAROLINA'S
BEACHES IN THE 1500S. LUCAS VÁZQUEZ DE AYLLÓN ESTAB-
LISHED THE FIRST EUROPEAN SETTLEMENT IN WHAT IS NOW
THE UNITED STATES IN 1526. THE SETTLEMENT WAS CALLED
SAN MIGUEL DE GUADALUPE. ALL BUT 150 OF THE 500 SET-
TLERS IN SAN MIGUEL DE GUADALUPE DIED A FEW MONTHS
LATER, INCLUDING AYLLÓN. THE SURVIVORS SOON LEFT.

French explorers built Charlesfort on one of South Carolina's outlying islands in 1562. But less than a year later, the town and most of its supplies were destroyed by fire. The desperate settlers sailed back home.

At the time of the European exploration, several American Indian tribes lived in South Carolina. The Cherokee, Iroquois, Sioux, Algonquin, and Creek had homes in the northern region. Smaller tribes, such as the Combahee and Kiawah, lived along the coast. They farmed the land, fished in the rivers, and collected pearls from the oysters in the ocean.

While the new settlers at Charlesfort found many American Indians to be peaceful (above), they also had to contend with attacks (opposite).

As the settlers came, however, the American Indians scattered. Some left to find new homes, but many died fighting the settlers. Others got sick from diseases, such as smallpox, brought by the Europeans.

YEAR

1562

EVENT

French settlers build Charlesfort on Parris Island but face starvation and are forced to leave within a year.

- 7 -

The first permanent European settlement in South Carolina was built by the English in 1670. It was named Charles Town (later spelled "Charleston"), after King Charles II. English settlers built plantations, or large farms. They brought slaves from Africa to plant and harvest rice. Many of the settlers became very rich. But life was dangerous. The settlers fought with the Indians. They also worried about pirates, who raided many ships coming into Charles Town. But it was the English government that became their worst enemy.

In 1765, England passed the Stamp Act, forcing the American colonies to pay taxes directly to the king in England. That angered the settlers. They fought for their freedom in the Revolutionary War, which started in 1775. Almost 140 battles of the war took place in South Carolina. When the war ended in 1783, the colonies formed the U.S. South Carolina became the eighth state to join the new country on May 23, 1788.

Although South Carolina was free, many of the people living there weren't. By 1850, at least 400,000 slaves worked on South Carolina's plantations. Many people in the Northern states thought slavery was wrong and wanted to end it. Most South Carolinians opposed that idea. In 1860, the state

The Americans won the Battle of Cowpens, which was fought in 1781 on South Carolina's northern border.

YEAR

1670 English settlers establish the state's first permanent European settlement at Albemarle Point.

EVENT

South Carolina's slaves were freed by Union soldiers as the Northern army swept through the South.

seceded, or left, the Union so that it could keep its slaves. Ten other Southern states that wanted slavery to continue also seceded. Together, they became the Confederate States of America.

The Civil War, which was fought between the North and the South, began on April 12, 1861. The first shots were fired from the Charleston Harbor on Fort Sumter, a Northern fort just off the South Carolina coast. The Confederate army won the first battle. But the North eventually overpowered the South. By the time the war ended in 1865, more than 15,000 soldiers from South Carolina had died.

South Carolina struggled to rebuild after the war. It also struggled to accept former slaves as free men and women. The effects of the Civil War were felt in South Carolina well into the 20th century.

Cities such as Charleston suffered greatly during the Civil War, with buildings and lives being destroyed.

YEAR

1729 The Carolina Colony splits to become North Carolina and South Carolina.

EVENT

- 10 -

Highs and Lows

South Carolina is shaped almost like a triangle. On the north, it borders North Carolina. It touches Georgia on the southwest. Its eastern border is the Atlantic Ocean. The coast stretches 187 miles (301 km) in a diagonal line from north to south. Counting all of the state's islands, bays, and

inlets, there are almost 3,000 miles (4,828 km) of beaches in South Carolina.

South Carolina has two distinct geographic regions, the Up Country and the Low Country. The northwestern part of the state is the Up Country. The Blue Ridge Mountains cross the corner of the state. Miners have found granite, topaz, and even gold in the mountains and in the rivers and streams that flow there. At 3,560 feet (1,085 m), Sassafras Mountain is the highest point in the state. From the top, mountains that are almost twice its size can be seen in the neighboring state of North Carolina.

South Carolina's coastline is known as the Low Country. The Low Country stretches from the ocean to the middle of the state. Parts of it are swampy and wet. Alligators, turtles, and snakes live in the wetlands. There are more than 40 kinds of snakes in the state.

From Caesars Head State Park (above) in the Blue Ridge Mountains to the beaches of Folly Island (opposite), the landscape offers highs and lows.

YEAR

1788   South Carolina becomes the eighth state on May 23.

EVENT

Cypress and oak trees grow in South Carolina's swampy areas. Strands of Spanish moss often hang from their branches. The state is also known for palmetto trees, which are common along the coastline. Farther inland, pine, magnolia, and hemlock trees heavily forest the land.

There are many peach trees in South Carolina as well. The state is one of the biggest producers of peaches in the country. The rich soil along the coastal plain is also good for growing cotton, tobacco, soybeans, and corn.

Beautiful flowers grow in South Carolina, too. In the spring, bright camellias, azaleas, jasmine, and black-eyed Susans bloom across the state. Venus flytraps, which trap and eat insects, also grow wild in South Carolina.

Among the state's plant life are wildflowers such as black-eyed Susans (above) on the mainland and forests of oak trees overgrown with Spanish moss in places such as Spring Island (opposite).

1790 The state legislature meets in the new capital of Columbia for the first time.

Hurricane Hugo devastated South Carolina's fishing industry when it struck the islands along the coast.

The Atlantic Ocean is important to South Carolina. Many people make a living catching shrimp. Tourists love the warm water and wide beaches. But the ocean also makes life danger-ous. South Carolina has been hit hard by hurricanes that start far out in the Atlantic.

One of the worst storms was Hurricane Hugo, which struck North and South Carolina in 1989. Hurricane Hugo's 135-mile-per-hour (217 km per hour) winds and heavy rains killed 56 people and caused billions of dollars worth of damage. Hundreds of trees were uprooted, and homes were destroyed. About 56,000 people were left homeless.

Even when hurricanes don't strike South Carolina, the state receives a lot of rain. An average of 48 inches (122 cm) of precipitation falls every year. Most of that is rain. Coastal areas receive less than an inch (2.5 cm) of snow each year. The interior might get about six inches (15 cm) in the winter.

Summertime temperatures in South Carolina can get as high as 100 °F (38 °C). Winters are very mild in South Carolina. Although parts of the Up Country can occasion-ally get below freezing, most of the coastal area stays warm. Average temperatures range from around 40 to 60 °F (4 to 16 °C). The weather is so nice that people can golf in South Carolina year-round.

When they aren't affected by bad weather, the state's outlying islands are popular vacation destinations.

YEAR
1860
EVENT
South Carolina is the first state to leave the Union over the issue of slavery.

Colorful Carolinians

WHEN EUROPEANS FIRST SETTLED IN SOUTH CAROLINA IN THE LATE 1600S, MANY AMERICAN INDIANS LIVED IN THE AREA. THEY ARE ALMOST ALL GONE NOW. MOST OF THE INDIANS WHO REMAIN LIVE IN THE MOUNTAINS ON A RESERVATION, WHICH IS LAND SET ASIDE FOR THEM BY THE U.S. GOVERNMENT.

Until the early 1900s, African Americans made up the majority of South Carolina's population. Their ancestors had come to the state as slaves. Today, African Americans make up about 30 percent of South Carolina's total population. A small number of Asian Americans and Hispanic Americans also live in the state, but about 70 percent of the population is white.

Relations between whites and blacks caused trouble in South Carolina for many years. Until 1948, most African Americans in South Carolina were not able to vote. White and black students went to different schools. The civil rights movement in the 1950s and '60s helped change that. Since then, South Carolina has tried to help everyone get along.

In the mid-20th century, blacks in Charleston were given the right to vote (above), and American Indians were educated in their own schools (opposite).

YEAR
1861   The first shots of the Civil War are fired on Fort Sumter from Charleston's harbor.
EVENT

- *19* -

Jesse Jackson became a Baptist minister in 1968, the same year in which Martin Luther King Jr. was killed.

There is still tension, however. A Confederate flag (which many people see as a symbol of division, from when the South and North were separated) flew at the state capitol in Columbia until 2000. Some people still struggle with the changes, but most of the state has embraced civil rights.

Jesse Jackson is an African American man who was born in South Carolina. Jackson began his career as a Baptist minister and helped civil rights activist Martin Luther King Jr. fight for equality in the South. Jackson later ran for president twice in the 1980s and traveled around the world to help many people solve their conflicts.

Another politician from South Carolina was Strom Thurmond. Thurmond ran for president in 1948 but lost. In

On January 21, 2002, protestors tried to get the Confederate flag removed from the grounds of the capitol.

YEAR

1868   South Carolina joins the Union again following the Civil War.

EVENT

1954, he was elected to the U.S. Senate. He was one of the longest-serving senators in history. Thurmond was 100 years old when he retired in 2003.

Jazz musician Dizzy Gillespie was born in Cheraw, South Carolina, in 1917. He played his trumpet with his cheeks puffed up with air. Gillespie helped invent bebop, a fast and complex style of jazz. Many people consider him one of the best jazz trumpeters ever.

Many well-known South Carolinians grew up living on or around cotton plantations. Most of those large farms are gone now. But farming is still important in South Carolina. The biggest crop today is lumber. Pine, oak, and maple trees are grown on commercial farms just to be cut down. Tree farms bring more than $650 million to the state every year.

Along with saxophone player Charlie Parker, Dizzy Gillespie is credited with the cofounding of bebop.

YEAR

1870

EVENT

Joseph Rainey becomes the first African American from South Carolina to serve as a U.S. Representative.

M

anufacturing also brings a lot of money to South Carolina. A BMW plant near Greenville makes expensive German cars. Other companies make airplanes, paper, clothing, and medical devices. More than 300,000 people work for manufacturers in South Carolina.

Many people also work in the tourism industry. They take care of the approximately 28 million tourists who visit South Carolina every year. Some work at hotels or resorts. Some work at restaurants or stores. Others work at golf courses or other recreational places.

People who visit South Carolina sometimes stay there permanently. The state's population is growing. For many years, more people lived in rural areas than in cities. Today, more people are moving to the state's cities. But there are still only two cities in South Carolina with more than 100,000 people: Columbia, the capital, and Charleston.

With a BMW manufacturing plant (above) that employs more than 5,400 people and prime vacation spots such as Hilton Head Island (opposite), the state offers good jobs and great fun.

A new dance craze called the "Charleston" begins to rage throughout the country.

Southern Charm

SOUTH CAROLINA'S LONG HISTORY MAKES IT A FASCINATING PLACE TO LIVE OR VISIT. THE STATE HAS WORKED HARD TO PRESERVE ITS PAST. THE CITY OF CHARLESTON IS A GOOD EXAMPLE. IT WAS THE FIRST CITY IN THE COUNTRY TO OFFICIALLY PROTECT ITS HISTORIC BUILDINGS.

More than 800 buildings that were built before the Civil War still stand in Charleston. Many of these buildings have been renovated to their original glory. Often, such buildings are open for tours. Tour guides dressed in period costumes tell stories from the past. Horse-drawn carriages also take visitors around the city to show off historic sites.

One favorite historic site in Charleston is Rainbow Row. Its name comes from the color of several row houses squeezed together in the city's downtown. The houses were originally built in the 1700s. In the early 1900s, residents decided to restore them. Now each one is painted a different color such as pink, yellow, or green.

African American culture is also an important part of South Carolina's history. The Gullah community keeps that culture alive. Gullah is the name of a language that combines African and English words. It also describes the group of people who speak that language.

A sense of history is preserved in Charleston's colorful Rainbow Row (opposite) and at the annual Gullah Festival (above) in Beaufort.

The Gullah community is made up of people whose ancestors were slaves. For about 300 years, they have lived and worked on the Sea Islands just off South Carolina's coast. They

YEAR

1963   Public schools in South Carolina are opened to both white and black students.

EVENT

have tried to keep the traditions of their African homeland alive. They teach their children to sing Gullah songs and tell Gullah stories. They make baskets and other traditional crafts. Their way of life is being threatened by building projects on the islands where they live, but fortunately, there are groups working with the Gullah people to preserve their culture.

South Carolina's islands and coast have also become known as great places to golf. There are more than 360 golf courses in the state. The best known are at Hilton Head and Myrtle Beach. Myrtle Beach, which has a population of about 25,000, has at least 100 courses. That means that there is one golf course for every 250 people in the city. The golf courses are open year-round. Many are located at beautiful resorts. They are some of South Carolina's most popular tourist destinations.

Professional golf tournaments are sometimes played on South Carolina's golf courses. But no professional sports teams play in the state. The Carolina Panthers football team represents North and South Carolina. The team trains in

South Carolinians may share their professional football team (opposite), but the pristine golf courses of Myrtle Beach (above) are their own.

YEAR

1989 Hurricane Hugo devastates South Carolina's coastline, causing $5 billion in damage to homes and property.

EVENT

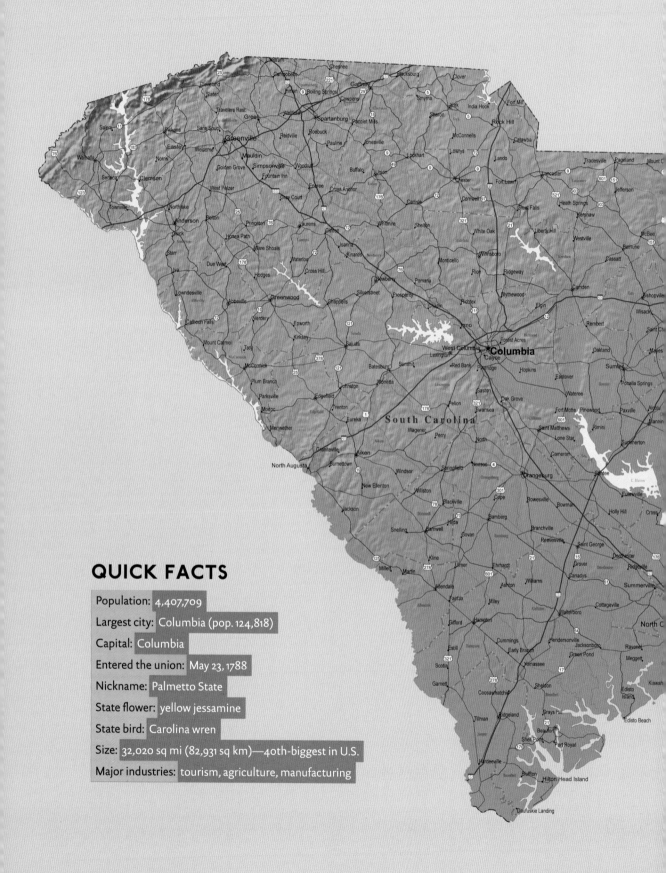

QUICK FACTS

Population: 4,407,709

Largest city: Columbia (pop. 124,818)

Capital: Columbia

Entered the union: May 23, 1788

Nickname: Palmetto State

State flower: yellow jessamine

State bird: Carolina wren

Size: 32,020 sq mi (82,931 sq km)—40th-biggest in U.S.

Major industries: tourism, agriculture, manufacturing

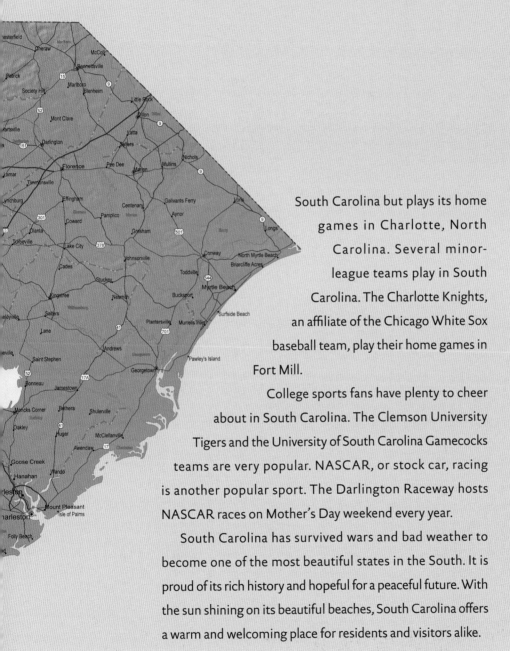

South Carolina but plays its home games in Charlotte, North Carolina. Several minor-league teams play in South Carolina. The Charlotte Knights, an affiliate of the Chicago White Sox baseball team, play their home games in Fort Mill.

College sports fans have plenty to cheer about in South Carolina. The Clemson University Tigers and the University of South Carolina Gamecocks teams are very popular. NASCAR, or stock car, racing is another popular sport. The Darlington Raceway hosts NASCAR races on Mother's Day weekend every year.

South Carolina has survived wars and bad weather to become one of the most beautiful states in the South. It is proud of its rich history and hopeful for a peaceful future. With the sun shining on its beautiful beaches, South Carolina offers a warm and welcoming place for residents and visitors alike.

YEAR

2003   Senator Strom Thurmond, a South Carolina native, retires from office at the age of 100.

EVENT

BIBLIOGRAPHY

Leifermann, Henry. *Compass American Guides: South Carolina*. New York: Compass American Guides/Fodor's Travel Publications, 2006.

Perry, Lee Davis, and J. Michael McLaughlin. *Insiders' Guide to Charleston*. Guilford, Conn.: Morris Book Publishing, 2007.

South Carolina Department of Archives & History. "A Brief History of South Carolina." State of South Carolina. http://scdah.sc.gov/schistory.htm.

Web Marketing Services. "South Carolina History Timeline." e-ReferenceDesk. http://www.e-referencedesk.com/resources/state-history-timeline/south-carolina.html.

Wright, Louis B. *South Carolina, A History*. New York: W. W. Norton & Company, 1976.

INDEX